Celebrations

Let's Get Ready for Hanukkah

By Joanne Winne

Welcome Books

Children's Press
A Division of Scholastic Inc.
New York / Toronto / London / Auckland / Sydney
Mexico City / New Delhi / Hong Kong
Danbury, Connecticut

Photo Credits: Cover and all photos by Maura Boruchow
Contributing Editors: Jeri Cipriano, Jennifer Silate
Book Design: Victoria Johnson

Visit Children's Press on the Internet at:
http://publishing.grolier.com

Library of Congress Cataloging-in-Publication Data

Winne, Joanne.
    Let's get ready for Hanukkah / by Joanne Winne.
        p. cm. -- (Celebrations)
    Includes bibliographical references and index.
    ISBN 0-516-23174-X (lib. bdg.) -- ISBN 0-516-29570-5 (pbk.)
    1. Hanukkah--Juvenile literature. [1. Hanukkah. 2. Holidays.]
    I. Title.
  BM695.H3 W56 2001
  296.4'35--dc21

                                              00-065623

Contents

Look at the **calendar**.

Today is a **special** day.

It is the first day
of **Hanukkah**.

Hanukkah is a **celebration** that lasts for eight days.

On the first night of Hanukkah, we light one candle on the **menorah**.

9

I help Grandma make potato pancakes.

Grandpa and I eat cookies.

Grandma plays the **dreidel** game with us.

We take turns spinning the dreidel.

Grandpa gives us **chocolate** coins.

19

Each night, we get presents.

This is how we celebrate Hanukkah.

21

New Words

calendar (**kal**-uhn-duhr) a chart showing the months, weeks, and days of the year

celebration (sehl-uh-**bray**-shuhn) a party or other activity on a special day

chocolate (**chahk**-liht) a sweet made from roasted and ground cacao beans

dreidel (**dray**-dl) a kind of spinning top

Hanukkah (**hah**-nuh-kuh) a yearly Jewish festival that lasts eight days

menorah (muh-**nor**-uh) a candlestick with eight branches

special (**spehsh**-uhl) extraordinary, exceptional

To Find Out More

Books
Is It Hanukkah Yet?
by Nancy E. Krulik
Random House

My Two Grandmothers
by Effin Older
Harcourt Brace

Web Site
Billy Bear's Hanukkah
http://www.billybear4kids.com/holidays/hanukkah/hanukkah.htm
This Web site has games, crafts, and e-cards for celebrating
Hanukkah.

Index

About the Author
Joanne Winne taught fourth grade for nine years. She currently writes and edits books for children. She lives in Hoboken, New Jersey.

Reading Consultants
Kris Flynn, Coordinator, Small School District Literacy, The San Diego County Office of Education

Shelly Forys, Certified Reading Recovery Specialist, W.J. Zahnow Elementary School, Waterloo, IL

Sue McAdams, Certified Reading Recovery Specialist and Literary Consultant, Dallas, TX